ABC
Amazing
Book of
Crystals

Fun Photos for Rock Lovers of All Ages

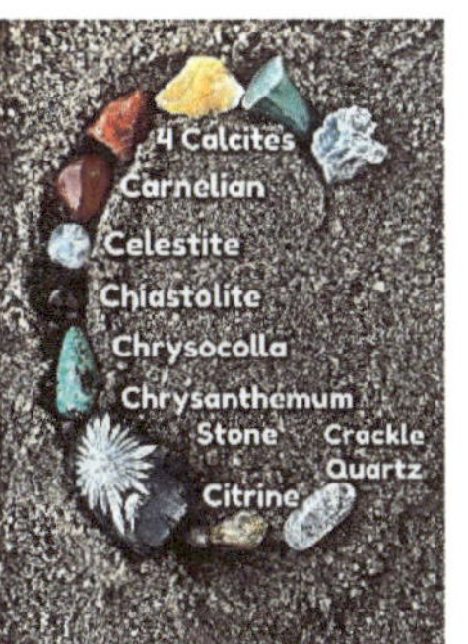

Brenda DeHaan

DeHaan, Brenda
ABC Amazing Book of Crystals: Fun Photos for Rock Lovers for All Ages

1. Rocks and minerals. 2. Geology.
3. Mineralogy 4. Science 5. Alphabet
552

Earth has thousands of cool rocks—more than you could count. This book has photographs of almost 200 stones (also called *crystals*) in alphabetical order. When you see rocks that you want to learn more about, check library books or online for more information. Maybe ask a family member, teacher, or librarian to help you research for information.

Do not worry if you do not know how to pronounce each rock's name. Some of them are tricky even for adults. Just focus on what it looks like.

Some rocks have gem qualities that make them perfect for jewelry. These stones often have inexpensive versions that could be part of your rock collection.

At the end of the book, decide which ones are your favorite crystals. Different rocks appeal to different people. Some pick by color, some go by shapes, and some like rocks for no special reason. There's a rock for everyone!

Can you see the letter **A**
in the sand?
Trace it with your finger.

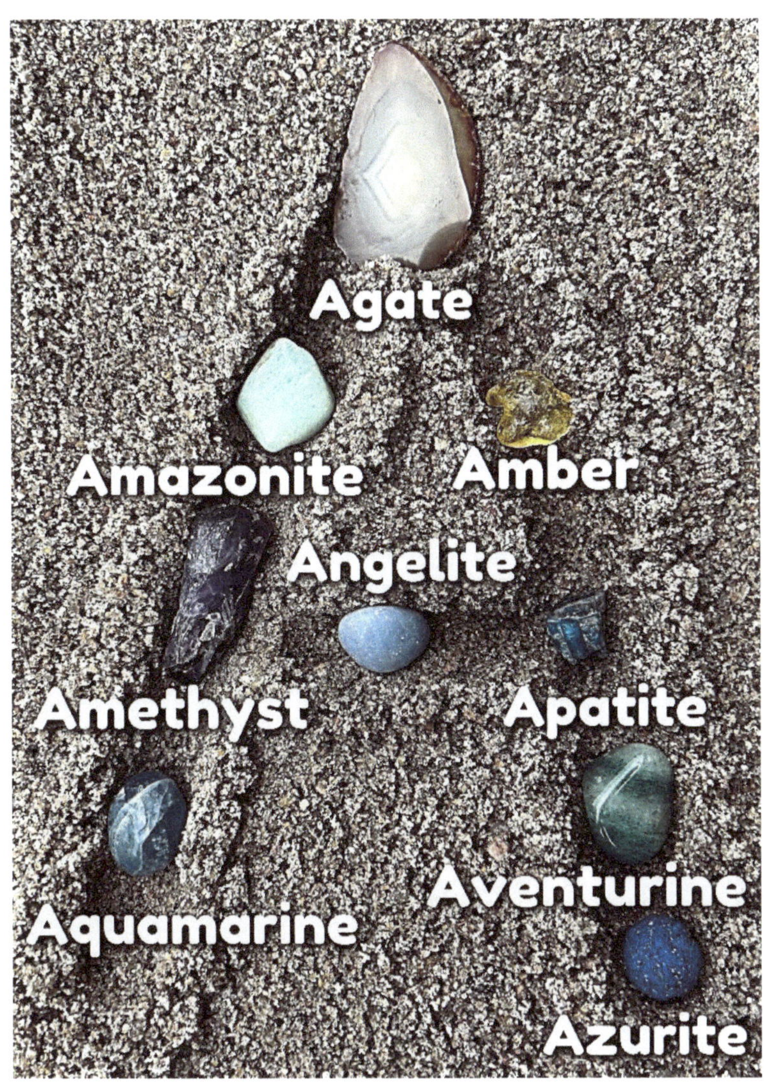

A isfor agate, amazonite, amber, amethyst, angelite, apatite, aquamarine, aventurine, and azurite.

Can you see the letter **B**
in the sand?
Trace it with your finger.

B is for banded agate, bloodstone,
blue lace agate, blue tiger's eye, bornite,
Botswana agate, and bronzite.

Can you see the letter *C*
in the sand?
Trace it with your finger.

C is for calcite, carnelian, celestite, chiastolite, chrysocolla, chrysanthemum stone, citrine, and crackle quartz.

Can you see the letter **D**
in the sand?
Trace it with your finger.

D is for Dalmatian stone,
dendritic agate, desert rose selenite,
and dumortierite.

Can you see the letter *E*
in the sand?
Trace it with your finger.

E is for emeralds and epidote.

Can you see the letter *F*
in the sand?
Trace it with your finger.

F is for fairy stone, flint, fluorite, and fuchsite.

Can you see the letter **G**
in the sand?
Trace it with your finger.

G is for garnet, goldstone, and green garnet.

Can you see the letter **_H_**
in the sand?
Trace it with your finger.

H is for halite, healer's gold, hematite, and Herkimer diamonds.

Can you see the letter *I*
in the sand?
Trace it with your finger.

I is for Iceland spar
and imperial topaz.

Can you see the letter **J**
in the sand?
Trace it with your finger.

J is for jade and jasper.

Can you see the letter **K**
in the sand?
Trace it with your finger.

K is for K2, kambaba jasper, kunzite, and kyanite.

Can you see the letter *L*
in the sand?
Trace it with your finger.

L is for labradorite, lapis lazuli, larimar, larvikite, leopardskin jasper, and lepidolite.

Can you see the letter *M*
in the sand?
Trace it with your finger.

M is for magnesite, malachite, mangano calcite, Mexican crazy lace agate, moonstone, and moss agate.

Can you see the letter **N**
in the sand?
Trace it with your finger.

N is for new jade and nuummite.

Can you see the letter *O*
in the sand?
Trace it with your finger.

O is for obsidian, ocean jasper,
onyx, and opal.

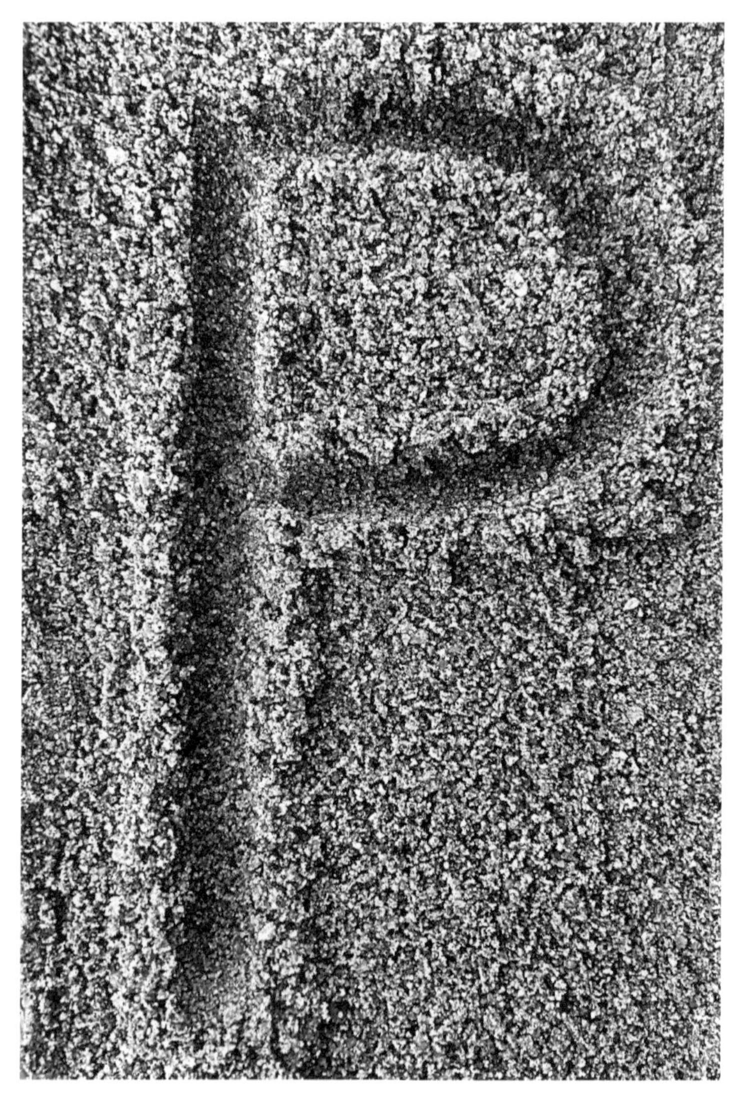

Can you see the letter *P*
in the sand?
Trace it with your finger.

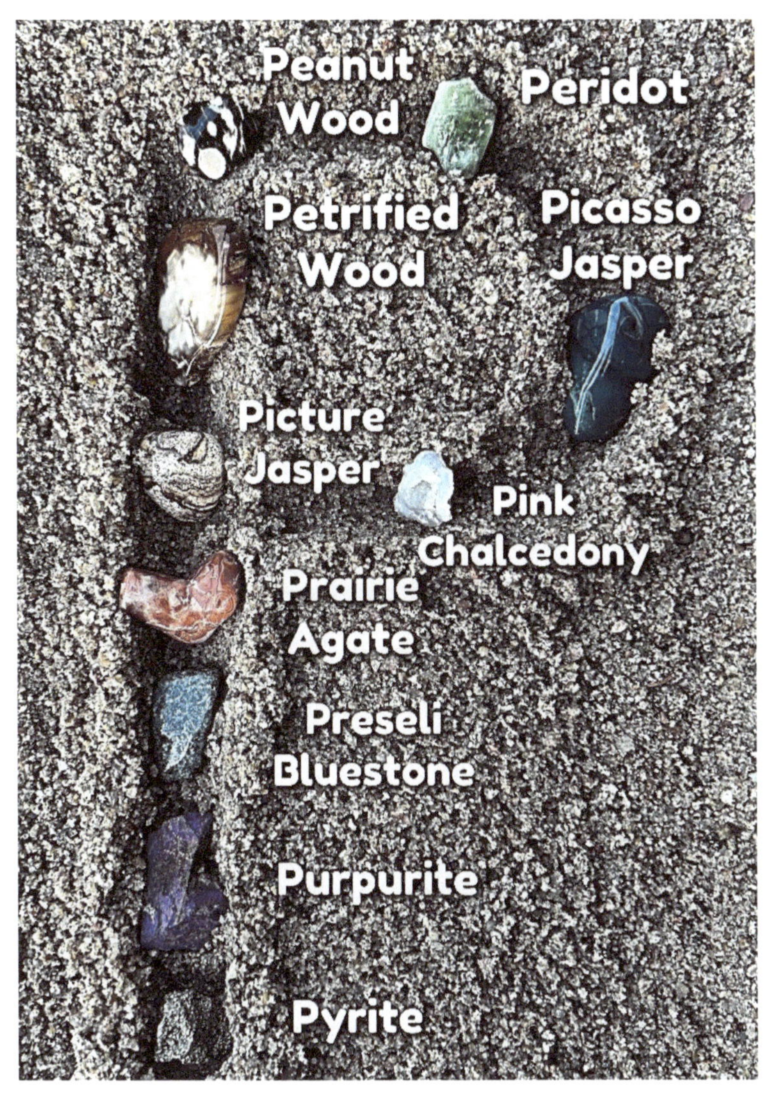

P is for peanut wood, peridot, petrified wood, Picasso jasper, picture jasper, pink chalcedony, prairie agate, Preseli bluestone, purpurite, and pyrite.

Can you see the letter *Q*
in the sand?
Trace it with your finger

Q is for quartz.

Can you see the letter **R**
in the sand?
Trace it with your finger.

R is for rainbow moonstone, rainforest jasper, red jasper, red tiger's eye, rhodochrosite, rhodonite, rose quartz, and ruby.

Can you see the letter **S**
in the sand?
Trace it with your finger.

S is for sardonyx, satin spar, scolecite, selenite, septarian, seraphinite, shiva eye shell, shiva lingam, shungite, smokey quartz, snakeskin agate, snow quartz, sodalite, spiderweb jasper, strombolite, and sunstone.

Can you see the letter *T*
in the sand?
Trace it with your finger.

T is for tektite, thulite, tiger's eye, topaz, tourmaline, tree agate, turquoise, and turritella agate.

Can you see the letter *U*
in the sand?
Trace it with your finger.

U is for ulexite and unakite.

Can you see the letter **V**
in the sand?
Trace it with your finger.

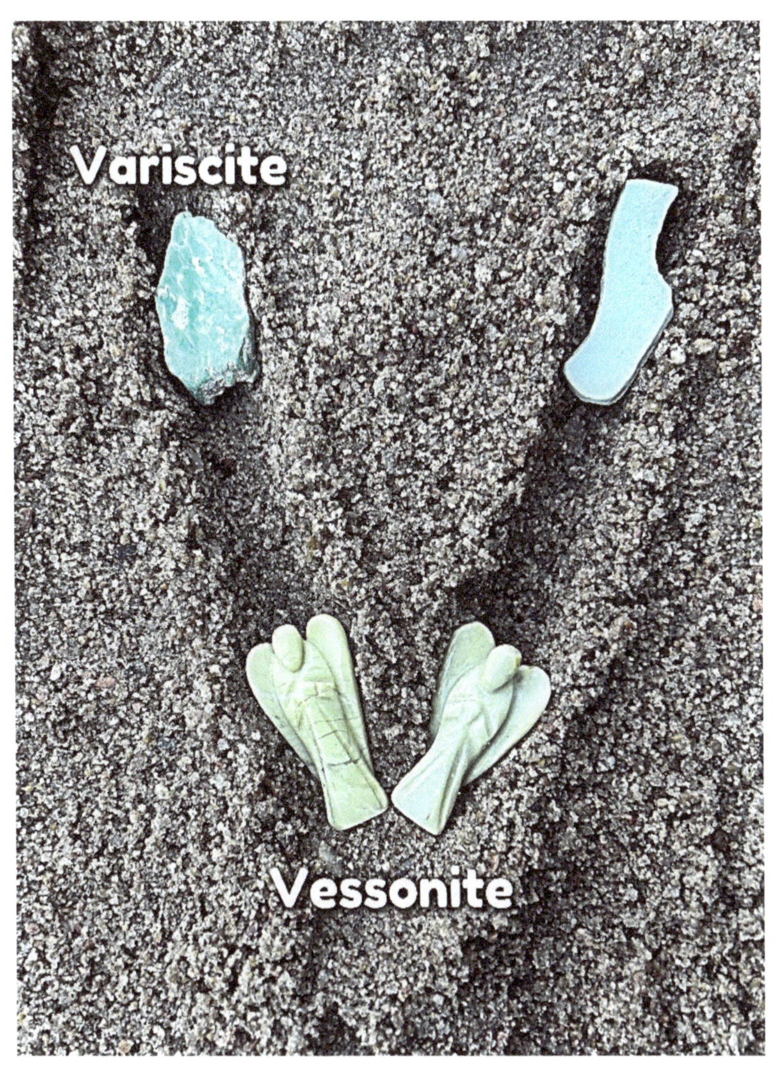

V is for variscite and vessonite.

Can you see the letter **W**
in the sand?
Trace it with your finger.

W is for wavellite.

Can you see the letter **X**
in the sand?
Trace it with your finger.

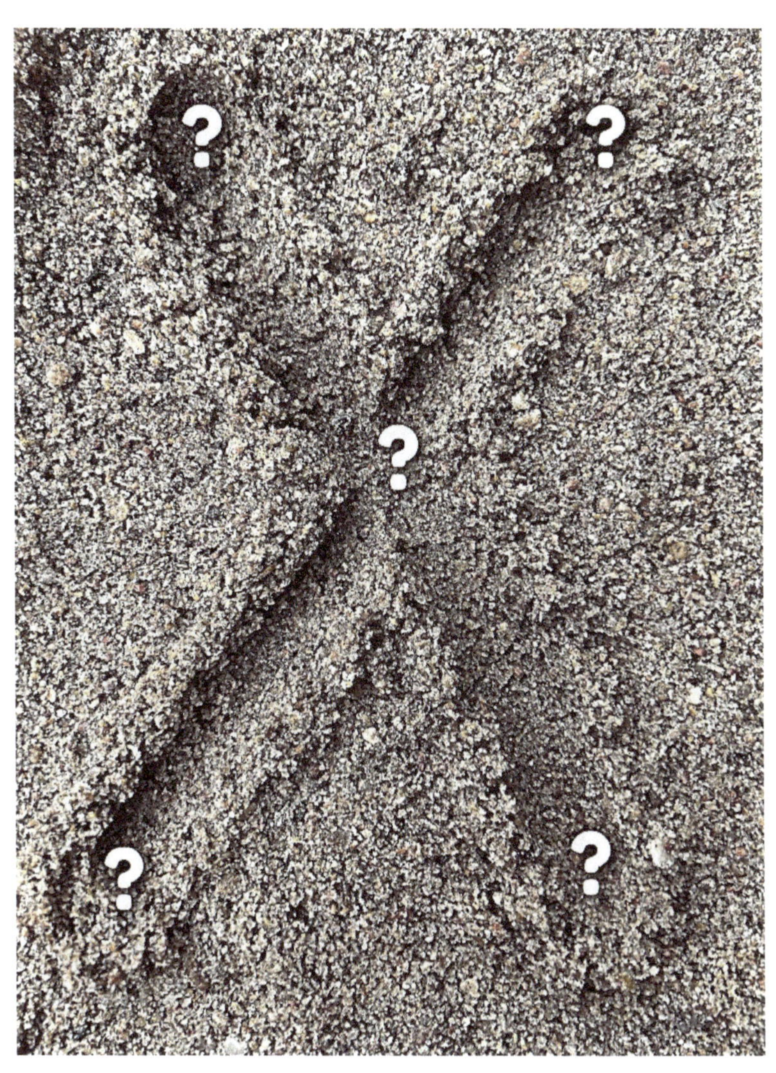

Hey! What happened to the rocks?
Maybe an **x**-ray machine made xaga,
xalostocite, xanthite, xenolith, and
xyloid jasper invisible!

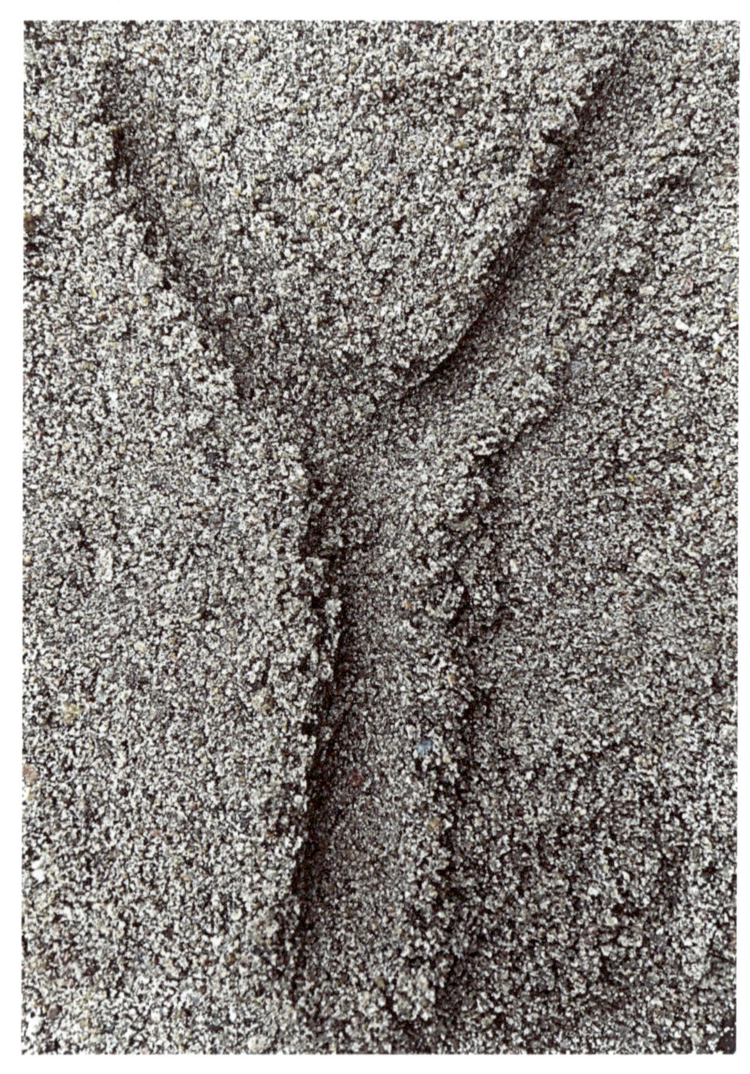

Can you see the letter **Y**
in the sand?
Trace it with your finger.

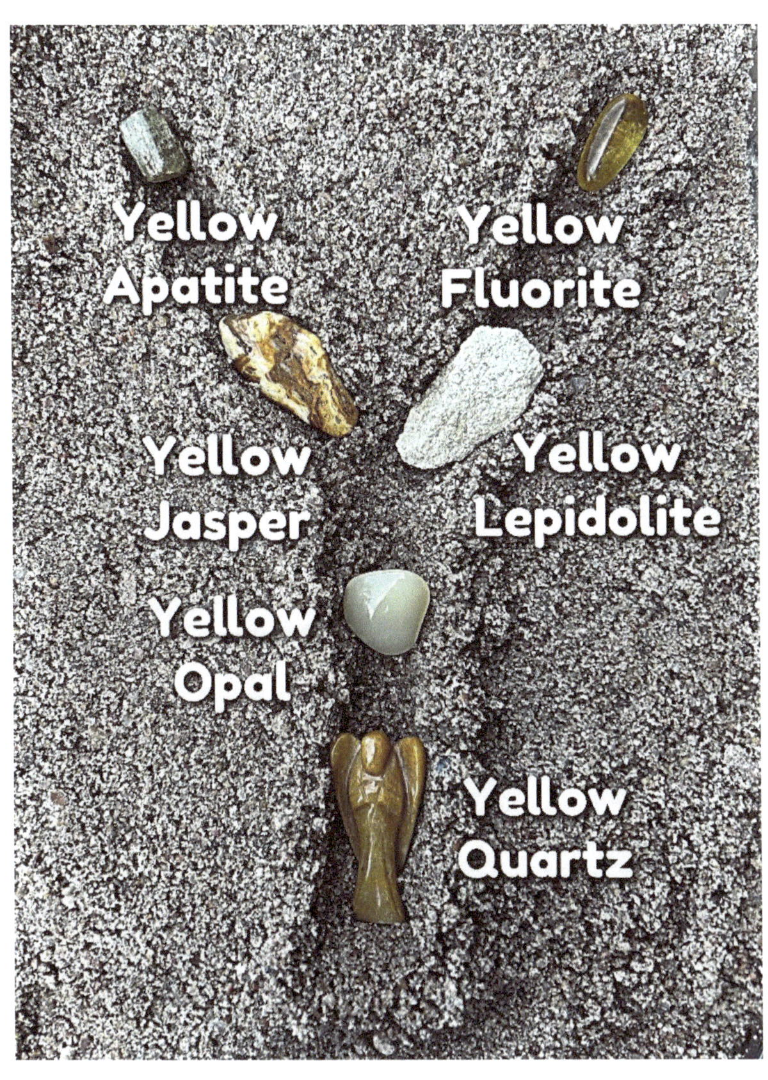

Y is for yellow apatite, yellow fluorite, yellow jasper, yellow lepidolite, yellow opal, and yellow quartz.

Can you see the letter **Z**
in the sand?
Trace it with your finger.

Z is for zebra moonstone,
zebra stone, and zoisite.

You have reached the end of the alphabet, but this could be just the beginning of learning more about rocks. When you think of your favorite rocks, which are the first ones that come to your mind? Find more information about those rocks.

If you want a rock collection of your own, start with cool rocks that you find in your neighborhood and state. Then when you visit other places, maybe you could find special rocks there or buy some in rock shops.

Another idea is to tell people what kind of rocks you would like for your birthday or for a holiday gift. People like buying presents that they know the recipient will love!

Since many rocks are found in other countries, the easiest way to get them is to buy them in a rock shop or online. You will not find those while searching outside.

The author started her rock collection when she went on a vacation in the Rocky Mountains and bought a chevron amethyst, a clear quartz, and a tiger's eye. That was just the beginning of a fun hobby of rock collecting. These three crystals are still her favorites!

About the Author

Brenda DeHaan is a K-12 librarian who loves rocks and reading. She hopes that you do also. This amethyst geode cathedral is the largest rock in her collection.

She is still searching for some crystals that start with the letter *x*.

Children's Books by Brenda DeHaan

***Rocks Rock**: Rough and Tumbled, Colorful and Cool Rocks and Minerals*

***The Flower Fairies Meet the Talking Rainbow Rocks**

***Beach Surprise:** Unicorns, Mermaids, Flower Fairies, and Rainbow Rocks Meet at the Beach*

***Crystals for Kids**: Learn the Names of 17 Rocks and Minerals*

***Hooray for a Fun Day!**

***Rocks with Socks and Fox**

***Rocks and Rhyme 2 in 1 Fun**: Crystals for Kids and Rocks with Socks and Fox*

***Adventures with Apollo**: The Cat Who Rules Rooftops*

***Abenteuer mit Apollo**

***Cat Naps, Dog Naps: Who Naps More?**

***From Apple to Zombie Drawing Challenge**: Illustrate Your Own Halloween Book*

***From Angel to Zzzz's Drawing Challenge**: Illustrate Your Own Christmas Book*

Tweens and Teens

***Shine Life a Crystal**: 12 Quick Tips to Rock Life*
***Life Advice for Teens from an Ageless Grandma**: Tips and Encouragement Just for You*

9 798852 793324